ROADMAP TO PUBLISHING CHILDREN'S BOOKS

A Step-by-Step Guide from Idea to Publication

Praise for ROADMAP TO PUBLISHING CHILDREN'S BOOKS

Packed with valuable information, Diana Aleksandrova's easy-to-follow book on self-publishing is the perfect step-by-step guide for anyone interested in the self-publishing process from start to finish. A must-have describing the ins and outs of the self-publishing world. She covers it all!

Judie Anderson Offeredahl, Elementary Educator and Children's Books Author

Diana Aleksandrova's "Roadmap to Publishing Children's Books" is an invaluable resource for anyone embarking on the journey of writing and publishing children's literature. From the genesis of an idea to the practicalities of publication, Aleksandrova offers a detailed, step-by-step guide that covers everything a self-published author needs to know. She delves into critical aspects like whether to write to market, the importance of drafting your ideas, and how to truly make your story shine.

Moreover, her insights into joining critique groups, the significance of editing, and the specifics of book orientation and trim size are particularly enlightening. What sets this book apart is Aleksandrova's practical advice on choosing an illustrator, understanding the costs involved, and navigating the essentials like Amazon Author Central, Amazon Ads, ISBNs, Library of Congress numbers, and copyrights. The use of checklists for writing and marketing, along with a comprehensive list of resources for new authors, makes this guide a must-have. It's a roadmap I wish I had at the start of my career, packed with wisdom that equips authors to navigate their publishing journey with confidence.

JoAnn Dickinson, Children's Books Author and Publisher

I have known and worked with Diana a long time as a beta reader and illustrator, so I know Diana is the right one to pen this reference guide. With a stellar background in award-winning self-published children's books, you can trust in her guidance as she takes you through the steps of writing, publishing, and successfully marketing your book. A solid must-read if you are serious about getting your self-published book into the hands of readers.

Victoria Marble Children's Books Author and Illustrator

Roadmap to Publishing was like a dialog with a good friend who knows a lot about how to create a successful book. In this book, Diana is sharing an obvious and inspiring roadmap on how to get your manuscript ready for editing, find an illustrator, copyright a book, publish, and get it into the hands of your readers. The steps described in the book are actionable and clear, even for a beginner in self-publishing, it is a joy to have such a book on my bookshelf to refer to every time I need to create a new book. I look forward to implementing the strategies described in this book and seeing where they lead us and our books.

Irina Trzaskos, Book Illustrator and co-creator of Tales From a Magical Forest Book Series.

I have so many ideas for children's books, but when I went online looking for information, I hit a roadblock. There was just so much information out there, most of it conflicting and more often than not, behind an expensive paywall in the form of unaffordable courses. Thank goodness for Diana Aleksandrova and her *Roadmap to Publishing Children's Books*.

This book is clear, easy to follow, and packed with useful information that covers everything from writing your manuscript to selling your book.

Even though I've written and self-published a few children's books already, I found this guide incredibly helpful. It's organized into five parts, making it easy to find the information I need, easily and quickly.

What I love about this book is that it's packed with great information, real-world examples, and practical advice. Whether you're a first-time author or an experienced writer, you'll find valuable information that you can apply right away.

I'll definitely be dipping back into this guide often. It has made the self-publishing journey much less daunting and has given me the confidence to share many more of my stories with the world. Thank you, Diana, for such a wonderful guide on publishing children's books.

Violet Meadows, Children's Author

It can be overwhelming to be a new writer trying to navigate the labyrinth of writing children's books. You join many groups, follow other authors, and get a lot of helpful advice. But sometimes, it gets all jumbled up, and you don't know what to prioritize and in what order to do things. Diana has written a book to clear the path for us so it makes so much more sense now. I now have a much clearer idea of what to expect and how to get there. Sometimes, you don't know what you don't know, and I know how to avoid some bumps on the road, and mostly, it doesn't feel as overwhelming anymore. If you're a brand-new writer and need some more clarity, this is a great book to check out!

Annie Smith

ROADMAP TO PUBLISHING is full of fantastic information. It is well researched and informative. Even those who have already self-published may learn something new. I appreciated how the author differentiates between publishing services and pricing available in different countries like Canada vs. USA.

Katie Baker, Author

This is the book you need when you are about to start out on your writing journey. It's also a useful guide for any writer who wants to review their writing plan. It is clear, concise, and written in a way that enables you to understand how your writing journey will progress.

You'll read it and wonder how you will ever get to write and publish your own book. There's lots of information, and it can be daunting, but remember, the journey of a thousand miles begins with the first steps. You don't need to ingest all this information at once. This book is a roadmap that will ensure you are guided along a well-trodden path. This book is a step-by-step guide that will keep you on a path to writing your own book and getting it published.

Teresa Bellamy, Author and Co-founder of The Elephant's Trunk

If you are interested in Children's literature, you need to get Diana Aleksandrova's new book Roadmap to Publishing.

Diana goes through the entire process in an easy-to-follow, step-by-step way that includes many valuable links and suggestions.

Tip - Get the paperback version over the eBook, so you have it at hand for reference.

Suzy Duffy, United Tales of America

Not only is the advice thorough, actionable, and concise, but this book is engaging and inspires me to get back to work! This has been one of the most valuable resources on my journey to being a published author.

EM Whitlock

Copyright © 2024 by Diana Aleksandrova

All rights reserved. No part of this publication may be reproduced, distributed, or transmitted in any form or by any means, including photocopying, recording, or other electronic or mechanical methods, without prior written permission from the publisher.

Hardcover ISBN: 978-1-953118-27-1

Paperback ISBN: 978-1-953118-30-1

Library of Congress Control Number: 2024914771

Published by Dedoni Books

ROADMAP TO PUBLISHING CHILDREN'S BOOKS

A Step-by-Step Guide from Idea to Publication

Diana Aleksandrova

CONTENTS

INTRODUCTION	1
WRITING A MANUSCRIPT	3
Chapter 1 Writing to Market or Not	5
Chapter 2 Write it Down!	8
Chapter 3 Make Your Story Stand Out Through Proven "Rules"	11
Chapter 4 Critique Partners and Groups	16
THE BUSINESS OF CREATING THE BOOK	21
Chapter 5 Build Those Connections	23
Chapter 6 Becoming a Business Owner	25
Chapter 7 Editing	28
Chapter 8 Orientation and Trim size	31
Chapter 9 Illustrations	34
Chapter 10 The Layout of Children's Books	40
Chapter 11 ISBN and Barcode, Library of Congress Number	42
Chapter 12 Copyright	48
Chapter 13 Designing and Formatting	50
PUBLISHING YOUR BOOK	57
Chapter 14 POD vs Offset	59
Chapter 15 Fundraising	63
Chapter 16 Print-on-Demand Options	64
Chapter 17 Ingram Spark Title Set-up.	67
Chapter 18 KDP Title Set-up	72
GETTING YOUR BOOK IN THE HANDS OF THE READER	79
Chapter 19 Selling on Amazon	81

Chapter 20 Selling Through Your Website	*85*
Chapter 21 Schools and In-Person Events	*86*
YOUR MARKETING PLAN	**89**
Chapter 22 Website	*91*
Chapter 23 Social Media	*94*
Chapter 24 When to Run Ads	*97*
Chapter 25 Email List	*99*
Chapter 26 Reviews and Launch Teams	*101*
Chapter 27 Pre-orders and Press Releases	*104*
RESOURCES	**107**

INTRODUCTION

"IF YOU DO WHAT YOU LOVE, YOU'LL NEVER HAVE TO WORK A DAY IN YOUR LIFE."

Nice thought, right? But let's be honest—it doesn't always pan out that way. Still, loving what you do surely makes the work more satisfying.

Who am I, and why am I qualified to write this book?
Great questions.
My name is Diana Aleksandrova. Over the last four years, I've successfully published twelve children's books. These have gained thousands of positive reviews on Amazon and won four different awards.

I won't bore you with how I started writing or my experience with traditional publishing. Suffice it to say it was disappointing, which is why I turned to self-publishing.

When I decided on the self-publishing route, I was clueless. I had to dive deep into research, ask a million questions, and lurk in countless Facebook groups to find all the needed information. Editing, illustrations, layouts, formatting, copyrights—you name it, I had to learn it. And believe me, there was a lot to learn.

This book is meant to be used as a manual or reference guide for each step of the self-publishing process. It includes everything I've learned and what you need to know to self-publish a children's book. Hopefully, I can cut some corners for you.

I've separated this process into a few steps—each with a designated section—which you can easily refer to later:

- I. WRITING A MANUSCRIPT
- II. CREATING YOUR BOOK
- III. PUBLISHING
- IV. SELLING YOUR BOOK
- V. YOUR MARKETING PLAN: Getting your book in the hands of readers

Downloadable templates and resources on writing, publishing, and marketing:
https://www.dedonibooks.com/resources

WRITING A MANUSCRIPT

(and making it the best it can be)

If you're reading this book, chances are you have an idea brewing or have already written your first story and decided on self-publishing.

So, let's kick in by exploring your idea and figuring out where it fits.

Chapter 1 Writing to Market or Not

What is writing to market?

Writing to market means considering the current trends and demands of the market before crafting your story. In other words, you write your story with the intention of meeting what's hot right now. I'm not a fan of writing children's books to market; I can't spit out on-demand content. Yet, this method works for many authors.

As of the writing of this book, there are several current market trends in children's literature. Diversity and inclusion books are in demand. Empowering stories and ones that help kids regulate emotions are popular, too. There are plenty of trends, and you can check that for yourself by going to the nearest Target or Barnes and Noble and looking at which books dominate the shelves. Amazon's best-seller rank is another valuable tool for researching hot trends.

Let's look at the advantages and disadvantages of writing to market.

If you write to market, you pick trends that are already in demand. There is an established market, and you don't have to figure out where your book fits.

It's easy to find categories to fit in. You can cash in on the current demand and gross a quick profit.

The negative side is that the market might already be saturated (or quickly becoming saturated). It is harder to write a quality story on demand.

By the time the book is ready for release, the market trend might have shifted, leading to a short shelf life.

Pros

Books are already in demand.

There is an established market. You don't have to figure out where your book fits.

It's easy to find categories to fit in.

Quick profit.

Cons

The market might already be saturated (or quickly becoming saturated).

It takes work to write a quality story on demand.

If you have an idea that fits a specific market trend, go for it. However, you must have a unique approach and quality writing to make your book stand out.

Discovering an untapped market niche is an entirely different ball game. If you're fortunate enough to hop on that train with a high-quality product, success will come much easier and faster.

Chapter 2 Write it Down!

If you haven't already, write your story down without worrying about making it the best it can be just yet. All stories go through numerous revisions. Not one will stay in its original draft. There's always a second, a third...and sometimes a fifteenth draft. You should never expect to write a perfect story on the first try.

Most writers fall into one of the following categories.

Naïvely optimistic: the one who believes that everything she writes is the best thing ever written (or at least very good) and ready to publish the minute the first draft is finished.

Self-doubting pessimist: the one who doubts her story so much that she would never let anyone read it and, in some extreme cases, has trouble putting it on paper because she doesn't think it's worth it. Self-doubt can be paralyzing. To be a writer, you must overcome your fears and plow ahead.

Methodical professional: the one who is a healthy mix of the first two. An author who recognizes a good idea and is prepared and willing to work to produce the best version of her story.

Don't get me wrong, not every story is meant to be published—or even written—but that's not what I'm talking about here. Some excellent writers doubt their work so much that it doesn't see the light of the day.

The first try is just the beginning. It's an essential step that you have to take.

Write it down. Write a story with a beginning, middle, and end, and aim for the proper word count for the intended age group (more on this below).

Then, work on improving it!

Is your story for the youngest listeners? Does it have twists and turns? Does it have engaging, relatable chapters? How old are your characters?

I have seen an interesting statistic suggesting the average word count for children's books has gone down. Is this because we have a shorter attention span, and the next generation is growing up looking for the instant gratification technology provides nowadays? Maybe so.

Let's take a look at the approximate word count for each main category.

Board Books: less than 200 (many are under 100 words)

Picture Books: 350–1000 (500 is the recommended sweet spot; remember less is more)

Early Readers: 1000–3000

Chapter Books: 4000–10000

Middle Grade: 20000–50000

These are only recommendations. Don't worry excessively about your word count at the beginning. Over time, you'll learn to cut the "fluff" and say more with less.

Chapter 3 Make Your Story Stand Out Through Proven "Rules"

Who knew there were rules when it came to writing for kids? I grew up reading European authors and had no idea what picture books were, the structure they followed, and the rules attached to them. I hate rules, so let's call them guidelines. You can decide which ones you want to follow and which ones you want to ignore. Remember, rules are flexible and ever-changing. Here are the most common ones when it comes to writing children's books. Consider this chapter a crash course on how to write children's books.

A lovable or relatable protagonist who solves his own problem

Kids must either like the character, feel for him, or identify with him. Parents can't solve the problem, and older siblings or friends shouldn't be solving the problem in the story either. Children love to be independent, and it's always good to empower them.

The rule of three

The protagonist has to try solving his problem three times before succeeding. Kids love patterns and repetitions. And yet, this is a rule I can take or leave, depending on the story. If the first attempt is engaging enough, the struggle is strong enough, or there is a twist, you might not need a second or third. It all depends on your story—does it need the rule of three or not?

Show, don't tell

That was hard to learn, and I envy authors who have mastered it. I like this rule. It makes writing more vivid. This rule can be used for emotions or actions. The simple way is to use stronger verbs and vivid dialogue where possible.
"John heard steps in the hallway. He hid as fast as he could under his bed."
Vs
"John's ears pricked at the squeaking of the old hard floors in the hallway. He dove under his bed."

The second one is much more engaging and fun to read. Keep it fun!

With Picture Books, we can show through the illustrations. However, the text should be noticed, as it can add depth and intrigue.

What is the difference between telling and showing? While telling is just labeling actions, emotions, situations, and places, showing paints a vivid picture, making the reader experience the action and feel the emotions. Instead of telling the reader what is happening, showing allows the reader to experience the story through the character's eyes and actions.

Use onomatopoeia

Onomatopoeia is a great way to bring your writing to life by mimicking the sounds associated with the actions or objects described.

Here is an example from MON-STAA:

"***Flap! Flap!*** The birds would fly away, scared of his matted coat."

Children love onomatopoeia. And most parents love reading books with onomatopoeia, which allows them to be more artistic. Onomatopoeia helps to create vivid imagery and can make the action in a story feel immediate and exciting. It also adds a fun, playful element to the text, encouraging children to participate in the storytelling process by mimicking the sounds. This keeps them entertained and aids in language development and phonetic awareness.

Onomatopoeia is an easy way to make your writing sing, though only use it if your story calls for it.

High stakes and surprises

Does your protagonist have a problem big enough? Is he facing a real danger? Or is he overcoming an obstacle that looks hard to conquer? How can you make it harder? Is the ending satisfying? Is it a surprise? The more times you answer "yes" to those questions, the better your story will be.

Cutting words

Remove all unnecessary adverbs or adjectives and instead use stronger verbs. Don't explain every little detail; there's no need to describe the surroundings or the color of the shirt the character is wearing unless they're a vital element of the story and not shown in the illustrations. Leave room for the illustrations—a lot can be shown through the art that can be omitted from the text. Leave out anything that's not essential or moving the story along.

Chapter 4 Critique Partners and Groups

Now that you've done your best with your story, it's time to see what others think.

My best advice is to join critique groups and find critique partners you can count on.

I have worked with numerous critique partners. When I say numerous, I mean easily over a hundred. With many, I have exchanged work on a one-time basis by answering a call for a critique in a Facebook group. Others stuck around, and we continued to work together. And a few became long-term, reliable partners. Not everyone will be your ideal critique partner, but you can learn a little bit from almost everyone—even if it's what you don't want to do with your story. Be willing to consider every suggestion, every advice, and each piece of constructive criticism. That doesn't mean accepting and changing your story. But it *does* mean weighing it and applying what feels right. It's your story, after all.

Facebook groups are a great place to meet people in different stages of their writing journey.
- *Sub It Club CRITIQUE PARTNER MATCHUP*—for all kinds of manuscripts
- *Sub It Club*—active for children's books. Not only can you find someone to critique your work, but also a lot of helpful information on writing.
- *KIDLIT411 MANUSCRIPT SWAP*—very active for Picture Books
- *The Writing Gals Critique Group*—mostly longer works

Those are just a few that I have used in the past. A simple search will reveal more.

If you're ready to invest in your work, here are two great ways of getting feedback.

12x12 Picture Book Challenge: an excellent way to get feedback from fellow authors who are serious about their craft. Also, they have monthly webinars, which are free for members.

SCBWI: you can post on their discussion board (called Blueboard) and get plenty of useful advice. I have seen stories there that later went on to get traditionally published. They also have free and paid webinars, which sometimes feature paid critiques from experts in the field such as agents and editors.

Plenty of other organizations offer classes, webinars, and paid critiques. I've tried quite a few of them with mixed results. If you want to try any of them, make sure you vet them first. Ask other authors what their experience was and if they would recommend them. That will save you money and time in the long run. I suggest sticking with the means I mentioned above.

A word on manuscript protection. Many writers worried that their work might get stolen. I have seen suggestions for copyrighting your manuscript at the beginning. But in my experience, it isn't plausible advice. The story goes through so many transformations that you, as the author, might not even recognize it at the end. I copyright my work at the final stage when it's ready for publication. That way, I copyright not only the text but the illustrations, too.

Copyright is automatically granted to you when you put that story on paper (or on your computer). Registering your work with the US Copyright Office further strengthens your rights in the event of a dispute.

Email the finished story to yourself, and you will have proof of when it was created.

One note here: the copyright law protects "original works of authorship," which can be literary works (books, poems, etc.), musical works, graphical works, and so on. However, it does NOT protect our ideas. Ideas are not copyrighted.

That said, I haven't heard of many cases of plagiarism in our writing community, and I hope you will never have to deal with it.

Writing the manuscript checklist:

First draft

Make sure the manuscript is within the standard word count for the genre

Revise your story

Find critique partners or groups

THE BUSINESS OF CREATING THE BOOK

And here is where you stop being an author and become an entrepreneur. You're starting a business. Publishing is a business, *your* business, and you'll wear many hats (unless you delegate some of the roles to others).

- Author
- Business owner
- Marketer
- Accountant
- Contract Specialist
- Researcher
- Social media coordinator

But don't worry—you'll still have fun on the way! Watching your story come to life is very exciting, and seeing your book in the hands of smiling kids is rewarding.

Chapter 5 Build Those Connections

You've written your manuscript. Now what? You've polished it as much as you can yourself. You've had it read and critiqued by others. You're pretty confident your baby is ready to see the world in the form of a book.

Great! Congratulations on the job well done! Most people don't even get that far, so a pat on the shoulder is in order.

It's time to prepare the ground for your launch. Start building those connections. Join Facebook groups for self-published authors if you haven't yet. Start socializing, learning, and building connections with other authors. Help them with their launches, back their Kickstarter campaigns if you have the means, and do whatever you can to be supportive and connect. I can't stress enough how important building these connections are—you can learn a lot from successful authors. They're also great resources when you start looking for editors and illustrators and doing your research on successful trends, styles, or cover designs.

Here are some Facebook groups with a wealth of information that helped me through my publishing journey.

- *Children's Book Authors and Illustrators: publishing, marketing and selling*
- *20BooksForKids*
- *Children's Book Author Community*
- *Publishing Children's Books: an Author Community*
- *Children's Book Author Social Media Marketing*

Chapter 6 Becoming a Business Owner

Now, it's time to start thinking as an entrepreneur. The next step for your manuscript will be editing. But set up your accounting before you hire and pay for an editor. Register a company and open a business checking account.

A little disclaimer is in order. I am not an accountant, and this chapter is not meant to give you legal advice. I am merely sharing my personal experience.

If you're reading this book, I assume you're serious about your publishing business and plan to publish more than one book.

Choose your imprint name. You want to look professional; this name will be shown on Amazon as the publisher's name (more on that later). My publishing name is Dedoni, or Dedoni Books, and it comes from a childhood nickname of mine.

Choosing between **sole proprietor** and **LLC** is a personal choice based on your long-term plans.

A sole proprietor is anyone who operates a business independently, even without registering as a business. Then, your legal name can be your business name, and you will be personally responsible for business debts. A sole proprietor is the least expensive business to register formally.

I registered an **LLC** because it provides greater separation between personal and company resources and offers higher protection for my personal assets. As a side note, do not mix personal and company accounts and resources because the protection mentioned below will be void. Use only one account or credit card to pay all your company expenses. Also, I was looking long-term, and LLC provides the option to have a few imprints under the same company (at least in Nevada). Another reason I decided on an LLC was the possibility of publishing other authors' books. The setup fees are higher, but I was willing to pay.

Open a business bank account, deposit funds, or dedicate a credit card to be used only for your business expenses.

Now that you have started your business, it's time to start spending money. Yay, the fun part (pun intended)!

Download the Publishing Checklist and Publishing Budget sheets and begin planning.

https://www.dedonibooks.com/resources

I will be adding more templates regularly to help all parts from your publishing journey.

Chapter 7 Editing

Your manuscript is written, critiqued, revised, and polished. It's ready to be sent to the editor.

But how do I find an editor? And what type of edit do you need?

Ask for recommendations in your Facebook groups. Don't go for anyone who recommends themselves; vet them with other authors.

Use professional websites like Reedsy. The editors there are vetted and have a long list of credentials and experience. You can get quotes from different editors and decide which one you can afford. Prices vary greatly and depend on the length of your story and the type of edit you need.

Types of Editing

Developmental edit—The big picture guru.

This is a professional critique. A good editor will give you feedback on your story's voice, character development, plot, strengths, and weaknesses. You'll get suggestions on improving the story and advice and ideas for revising it. This type of edit is meant to strengthen your story and make it the best it can be. This is also where a good editor makes a huge difference. Do not skip this part.

I have used numerous editors for this part, but not all are equal. I found the ones I like to work with on Reedsy, and they have experience with major publishing houses.
I highly recommend you use more than one editor with experience in children's books.

Copyedit: the line-by-line edit
This editor checks for consistency in voice, word choice, sentence structure, and basic grammar, improving the flow of the text.

Rhyme Editor
If your book is written in rhyme, you'll need a rhyme editor, a specialized wizard who ensures your verses flow like a well-oiled Dr. Seuss machine. When I penned "Mother's Love," my rhyme editor swooped in to fix my awkward couplets and off-beat stanzas. I'll admit I'm a little tone-deaf, and let's face it, no matter how cute, my accent doesn't help either.

Proofreading

This is the final stage after all other issues are addressed. The goal is to polish the text by correcting spelling, punctuation, and grammar. After this stage, the text should be ready to publish.

For your first book, you need all three types of editing! Don't skip that part!

It's not just about having these editors; it's about finding the right ones. Your editor should understand your vision and share your enthusiasm for your story.

When working with editors, you should be open to constructive criticism, but that doesn't mean you have to agree to every suggestion. You're the author, and you know the heart of your story. Seeking another opinion if you're unsure is always an option—that might be another editor, or you can go back to your critique partners.

Chapter 8 Orientation and Trim Size

Before hiring an illustrator, one crucial step is deciding on your book's orientation and trim size. The orientation is the shape of your book, and the trim size is precisely that: the size of your book. Those are important factors that influence the overall design and reader experience.

For chapter or middle-grade books, the standard orientation is portrait. This vertical format is familiar to readers and fits comfortably in their hands. Typical sizes for these books include:

- 5x8 inches
- 5.5x8.5 inches
- 6x9 inches

These dimensions are listed with the first digit representing the width and the second digit representing the height. Choosing between these sizes depends on your content and target audience. For instance, a slightly larger size, like 6x9, might be more appropriate for chapter books with more illustrations or larger text.

The options for picture books are more varied. They can be portrait (vertical), landscape (horizontal), or square.

Deciding on the orientation depends largely on the nature of your illustrations and the story you want to tell. Here are some guidelines:

Square Books: perfect for character-driven stories with illustrations focusing on characters and their interactions. The square format provides a balanced space for text and images, making it versatile and appealing. This format has become increasingly popular.

Landscape Books: best for panoramic, visually rich content. If your story involves wide scenes, such as landscapes or detailed backgrounds, the landscape orientation will enhance the visual experience.

Portrait Books: ideal for traditional storytelling and sequences that benefit from a vertical flow. This format is also more common and familiar to readers, making it a safe choice for many types of stories.

If you plan to use print-on-demand (POD) services, remember that they're more restricted in the sizes they can produce. Most POD presses can handle sizes up to 8.5x8.5 inches. If you want to print a book larger than this, you'll need to opt for bulk offset printing. Offset printing allows for greater flexibility in size and typically offers better quality and cost-efficiency for larger print runs.

A practical way to help decide on the orientation and size of your book is to visit your local library and explore the children's section. Observe the different formats and sizes of books. Note which ones attract your attention and why. Consider how the illustrations are presented in various orientations and how the size of the book enhances or detracts from the story.

By carefully considering the orientation and size of your book, you can ensure that your illustrations and text are presented in the best possible way, enhancing the reader's experience and the overall impact of your story.

Chapter 9 Illustrations

While you wait for your edits to return, begin searching for illustrators. Facebook, Instagram, and Upwork are all good places to check out.

Decide on a style. Do you want one that's popular today? What style fits your story? Are you looking for whimsical pencil-drawn illustrations, or do you prefer watercolor for your book?

Another good way to find an illustrator is to check books published by small independent presses and contact their illustrators if you like their styles. A fair warning: most good illustrators are booked for months ahead. You can still get lucky, but remember, you might have to wait. You can use the time to work on your social marketing and find groups and ways to connect with your target audience—the parents buying your books.

Vet your illustrators the same way you would an editor. Be aware of the numerous scams: Illustrators sometimes use stock or AI-generated images, and some will rip off others' portfolios and present them as theirs.

Illustrations and design

Illustrators play a vital role in the success of the book. They must be skilled artists and understand the unique structure of picture books.

The design of picture books is a crucial aspect that significantly impacts the appeal and effectiveness of the story. While most experienced illustrators know how to plan a picture book, those who just now begin working on books might need to become more familiar with storytelling. That is why you need to discuss your book's design and structure with your illustrator in advance.

It is important to vary the types of illustrations within a book, incorporating double spreads, single spreads, and spot illustrations. Double spreads are suited for expansive scenes or pivotal moments in the story and can create a dramatic effect. Single spreads focus the reader's attention on a specific part of the narrative, while spot illustrations can add charming details and break up the text, keeping young readers engaged.

Balancing between illustrations and text is a fine art that can significantly improve the experience for little readers. A well-designed picture book with diverse and thoughtfully placed illustrations ensures a dynamic and immersive reading experience.

Illustration prices

Be prepared to spend the majority of your budget here. For a quality product, you pay a premium price. The more popular your illustrator is, the higher the price, too, but you also pay for their name and following here. Prices can differ from $35-50 per page to $250-300 per page. Some will give you an offer "per book.". It all depends on the illustrator's experience and popularity. Illustrators who live in countries where the average wage is lower come with a lower price tag. Since everything is digital today, you will receive your illustrations by email, and payment is sent with the click of a button; it doesn't matter where your collaborators are located. I've been lucky to work with a few illustrators from abroad with no issues, but you have to do your homework and vet them before you commit.

Illustrators deserve to be paid well for their time and work, just like anyone with a different profession. Be wary of overly low prices. They often indicate stolen art or clip art. Make sure the portfolio you see is original works. Be honest and open about your budget. Create a trustworthy relationship with your illustrator. It goes a long way!

I have seen authors offering to pay illustrators as low as $200 per book, which seems not only naïve and unprofessional, but some might find it insulting. Real art takes time and effort, just like any other job. If you offer a low amount, you may still find people, but—unless those are students trying to build up a portfolio—the quality you receive will not do your book any justice.

Illustrations are what will sell your book. When it comes to children's books, the art is as important (and some will say more important) than the story itself. Here, it's especially true that a book is judged by its cover! I can't tell you how many times I've ordered books based on the covers and the style of the illustrations.

Be willing and prepared to **invest** a reasonable amount on illustrations.

Royalty or one-time payment

The two common ways to pay an illustrator are a set one-time payment (per page or per book) or a percentage of the sales. A hybrid solution also exists—a smaller upfront payment and a percentage of the sales.

This is entirely between you and your illustrator. Most artists will ask for a one-time payment because there is no guarantee that your book will sell enough to earn them royalty. I never do royalty contracts because of the added headache of tracking sales and the accounting involved with royalties.

Always have a signed contract!

Things to include in the illustration contract:

Scope of the work: here, you state that you agree that the illustrator will deliver an original work he created following your requirements and liking. Describe the scope of the project—name, approximate page count, how many single-page, double spread, or spot illustrations will be needed, and the negotiated price.

Time frame: allow ample time. Art takes time, and you have to be reasonable. If someone promises a quick turnaround, you should be wary.

Rights: do you receive a perpetual, exclusive license or, in other words, full rights over the illustrations? This means you can use the illustrations not only for the book but also modify and sell the images on merchandise if the opportunity arises. Or do you get a limited license, allowing you to use the illustrations in the book and for promotional purposes only? Those are important points to discuss and include in the contract.

The rights of credit: this is a separate point because no matter the above agreement, the illustrator has the right of authorship credit.

Payment: When and how is the payment sent? I have had contracts to pay after each illustration is received, in a few installments, or at the end of the book. Do not pay in front, especially if you do not have an established work relationship with the artist.

Delivering the files: how will they be delivered? And what type of file? PDF, PSD, etc.

Chapter 10 The Layout of Children's Books

Let's start with the layout of a traditional 32-page Picture book.

The book consists of:

Cover: self-explanatory

End sheets (for Hardcovers): with POD, there's no option to customize this. They're white and cannot be omitted. The end sheets keep the binding together. You can choose printed end sheets with offset print, making the book more attractive.

Page 1 – Title Page: think of this as a second cover. I would use a different illustration from the one on the main cover.

Page 2 – Copyright Page: copyright notice, LCCN, author, illustrator, editor (optional), edition number, and publisher and contact information.

Page 3 – Dedication page: this is optional. You can use "This book belongs to…" instead of dedication.

Page 4: – start of the book.

Page 31: – last page if you use POD.

Page 32: – last page if you use offset print.

Of course, some variations exist, but this is an excellent basic layout for Picture Books.

Longer works like Chapter Books and Middle Grade have a Content Page and are typically printed in black and white.

Chapter 11 ISBN and Barcode, Library of Congress Number

You will need a few things before you can put your book together.

ISBN
Each format needs its own ISBN.
You need one for Hardcover and one for Paperback.

This is from the site of Bowker, the official seller of ISBNs for the US: *"The purpose of the ISBN is to identify one specific version of a book. If you wish to have a print (hardbound or softbound) or electronic (ePUB, PDF, or MOBI) version, or even register a new version, you will need a unique ISBN for each format."*

That said, digital books do not need ISBNs—using one is optional, and I chose not to bother with one. I do not see an upside to having one.
Ingram Spark and Kindle Direct Publishing (KDP) both offer free ISBNs.

I do NOT recommend using theirs.

I recommend only buying ISBNs from the official seller—in the US, this is Bowker.

That way, you own your ISBN and can use the same number for your offset print run and every POD platform you choose to utilize (providing you're printing the same format.)

Do not buy ISBNs from resellers, other authors, publishers, or anyone else. ISBNs are not transferable. If you use one you get from someone other than the official seller, that entity will be considered the publisher, which means you gave away the rights to your book. Getting back those rights and dealing with Amazon can be a tremendous hustle.

Bowker offers a discount if you purchase more than one ISBN.

Website: https://www.bowker.com/isbn-us

Currently prices:
Single ISBN - $125
10 ISBNs- $295
100 ISBNs- $575
1000 ISBNs -$1500

Other countries:

UK - The Nielsen ISBN Agency for UK & Ireland is the only authorized seller of ISBNs.

Website: https://www.nielsenisbnstore.com/Home/Isbn

Current prices:

Single ISBN - £91.00

10 ISBNs- £169.00

100 ISBNs- £379.00

1000 ISBNs - £979.00

If you're in **Canada**, you're in luck. ISBNs are free for Canadian publishers. You can apply for one through the Library and Archives Canada.

Thorpe-Bowker® is the ONLY official source of ISBNs in **Australia**.

Website: https://www.bowker.com/isbn-au

Currently prices:

Single ISBN - $44

10 ISBNs- $88

100 ISBNs- $480

1000 ISBNs -$3035

I can't possibly cover every country in this book. If you're located in a country other than the ones above, do a simple search online and ensure you order from the official agency in your county, not a reseller.

If you're planning to create and publish more than one book—or even if it's only one book but you're offering Hardback and paperback—it makes sense to purchase in bulk.

Barcode

The barcode is just a graphic representation of the ISBN. You can obtain one for free from online generators. I like to use https://bookow.com/afteremailbarcode.php.

They do accept donations, which is always nice to do, especially if you use them a lot.

Do pay for ISBN!

Do not pay for a barcode!

Library of Congress Control Number

You need to obtain the Library of Congress Control Number (LCCN) from The Library of Congress, which goes on your

Copyright Page. Once your book is published, you must mail a copy to the Library of Congress. The book is only added to the library catalog after it's received there.

This step is optional, but I recommend it for two reasons.

First, librarians use this number to locate books in the national database. Having one will be helpful if you wish to get your books in public libraries.

Second, having your book cataloged in the Library of Congress serves as double insurance against plagiarism, in addition to copyrighting your book (see next section).
Some even believe it has the same power as a copyright.
I like to do both copyright and LCCN.

How to obtain LCCN:
You need to register for the Preassigned Control Number (PCN) program of the Library of Congress.

Here is the link:
https://www.loc.gov/publish/pcn/news/index.html

Or search the internet for "PrePub Book Link," and you will get there.

You will use the Author link even if you publish under your company name. Register and fill in a request for your book. Once you receive the email with your LCCN, you will include it on your copyright page. LCCN has no fee, but you must mail a book to the Library of Congress once it's published.

Chapter 12 Copyright

A note on copyright: your work is automatically copyrighted. You own the copyright to your book the moment you begin writing it. Registering it with your local copyright authority is just an additional safeguard measure.

Once you have all the files ready, generate a proof PDF copy and submit it to the US Copyright Office.

https://www.copyright.gov/registration/

The fee is $65 (text and illustrations); if you submit more than a month before publication, you can upload digital files instead of sending print copies. Take advantage of that option.

The certificate will arrive in 1-3 months.

Things to keep in mind:

What copyrights do you have? If you're the author, you automatically own the copyright for the text. If you have a written contract transferring the full rights of the illustrations to your name, you claim those, too. If the illustrator keeps the rights, you must register those in his or her name, which should also be noted on the copyright page.

In **Canada**, copyright is registered online through the Copyright Office, part of the Canadian Intellectual Property Office. The current fee for online registration is $50.

In the **UK** and **Australia**, there isn't an official copyright register. The books are automatically copyrighted.

Once you have all of that, you can finally put your book together.

Chapter 13 Designing and Formatting

Designing the cover

A well-designed cover is a must for a successful book.

Often, you have only one chance to make a first impression, and since shoppers on Amazon decide in less than 3 seconds which book to click, you have to make that impression count. Your book will compete with millions of other books. It has to stand out! Shoppers see the cover, title, and subtitle. And they will only read your title if the cover is enticing enough to grab their attention.

Is your illustrator versed in cover design? You might not need a cover designer if you have a good illustrator. If not, hiring a cover designer might be a good idea—in fact, I recommend it.

Formatting the Cover

You will need different files for the hardcover and the paperback.

When designing your children's book, understanding bleed and margins is essential to ensure a professional and polished final product.

Bleed refers to the area beyond the edge of where the paper will be trimmed. This ensures that your artwork or background color extends all the way to the edge of the page without leaving any unprinted white spaces. Typically, you should add an extra 0.125 inches (3mm) to each side of your document for bleed.

Margins are the safe zones within the trim area where important content like text and key elements of your illustrations should be placed. Keeping crucial content within these margins ensures that nothing gets cut off during trimming. Standard margins usually range from 0.5 to 0.75 inches, depending on the size of your book and your printer's preferences. By properly setting bleed and margins, you can avoid common pitfalls and ensure that your book looks polished and professional when printed.

Download the templates from Ingram Spark (hardcover and paperback) and KDP (paperback) and give them to your illustrator or formatter. It will be much easier for them to do it right from the beginning than trying to adjust the files to the templates later on. Using the templates for Ingram Spark is important! They have an outdated system that prevents you from previewing the files immediately. You have to wait for them to create Proof Copies, which might take days. If you don't get your files right the first time (I rarely do), it might take a couple of weeks or more of tweaking to get them looking as you intend. This is wasted time. The fewer changes you make, the better! Follow the instructions for the inside pages and use the cover templates.

Formatting the Inside Pages

I recommend offering your customers all formats available—hardcover, paperback, and Kindle. Unless you're doing a Kickstarter and printing, offset a large quantity. In that case, you can postpone offering the paperback (assuming you're printing hardcover for your fundraiser) and push to sell the books you already have in hand.

Most parents say they prefer the more durable hardcover edition for their kids. The obvious reason is that kids' books are read repeatedly and must last longer. The hardcovers protect the inside pages from the curious little hands—or feet, in some cases. But in recent years, paperbacks have been gaining popularity mostly because of their lower price. I sell many more paperbacks than hardcovers. Kindle books, on the other hand, are offered primarily for promotional purposes—more on that later.

Look up the requirements regarding margins. Here, the file for the hardcover and the paperback is mostly the same. The only difference is the ISBN on the copyright page. Don't forget to change that for each edition. I usually include both ISBNs in each edition, so I don't need to worry about messing up the numbers.

Here's a sample of the copyright page:

Text copyright © (YEAR) by (AUTHOR'S NAME)

Illustrations copyright © (YEAR) by (ILLUSTRATOR'S NAME)

All rights reserved. No part of this publication may be reproduced, distributed, or transmitted in any form or by any means, including photocopying, recording, or other electronic or mechanical methods, without prior written permission from the publisher.

Hardcover ISBN:

Paperback ISBN:

Library of Congress Control Number:

Published by (PUBLISHER'S NAME)

Once you have the PDF files for the print books, you can create a MOBI file for your digital book with **Kindle Kids**

Book Create. The program is free to download and very user-friendly. You can include custom links to your website or another of your books on Amazon or ask readers to sign up for your newsletter.

I like customizing my digital book's beginning and end to fit better on the screen. For example, I would center the Title Page to be seen in the middle of the screen instead of showing a half page on the right side of the screen. Little details like that make you look more professional and enhance the reader's experience. I have gotten more than one positive review pointing out that my books are well presented on Kindle devices.

A note on formatting

Can your illustrator format the book and inlay the text in the illustrations? This is where your skills might come into play. Do you have an eye for design? If so, you should learn basic formatting skills. I was sure I could never do this, and I was consequently surprised by how easy it was to learn. Each different printer requires a slight tweak of the cover file. The ones I work with have the same requirements for the inside pages. I'm not saying to do all the work by yourself, but being able to make slight tweaks instead of waiting on your illustrator or designer is cheaper, faster, and more convenient. Do so only if you're comfortable with your skills.

Adobe InDesign is the industry standard in book publishing. Many people use **Canva.com** or **PowerPoint** to format their books.

I prefer Photoshop ($9.90 per month) for picture books to inlay the text in the illustrations. I use Affinity Publisher to include the illustrations in the text for my chapter books. I find Affinity Publisher much easier to master than InDesign. With only a one-time payment of $49, it's a much more affordable program with great futures. I used Affinity to format this book.

Put your time into learning to use any of those programs, and it will pay off. It helps when you don't have to ask your illustrator or designer to make every minor change. The text needs to be moved a little to the right. You found a missing comma. The illustration of one of the pages needs to be moved so an important detail isn't cut in the middle where the two pages meet. Those are easy fixes that even technology-challenged people like me can learn to do. It saves time and money.

Creating the book checklist

Professional editing—developmental, line-by-line, proofreading

Decide on trim

Illustrations

ISBN and barcode

Library of Congress Control Number

Copyright

Designing and formatting the cover

Formatting the inside pages

PUBLISHING YOUR BOOK

In this part, we will look at the different print options and how to decide which is best for you. Included is a detailed step-by-step guide on how to set up your book with two of the most popular print-on-demand presses.

I have created a Publishing Checklist, which will help you keep everything organized. You can download it at: https://www.dedonibooks.com/resources

Chapter 14 POD vs. Offset

When it comes to printing, there are two main options available to you—print on Demand (POD) and printing in bulk.

With POD, books are printed once the company receives an order. The process is automated and maintenance-free for the publisher (you; you're a publisher now). There is no garage full of books and no option to run out of stock.

Printing in bulk can be digital or offset. Digital printing and offset printing are two distinct methods with their own advantages. Digital printing is ideal for short runs, offering quick turnaround times and easy customization without the need for printing plates. In contrast, offset printing is more cost-effective for large print runs, producing high-quality, sharp images, but requires a longer setup time and initial costs. While digital printing excels in flexibility and speed, offset printing is preferred for its consistency and economy in high-volume jobs.

The prices are higher with digital presses, but you can order just a few copies, while the minimum with offset press is usually 1000 books.

I'll use offset printers for comparison purposes and the rest of this book.

Before you proceed, you must decide how to print and ship your books to your customers. You have to choose between the convenience of Print on Demand and the potentially higher profit margin and better offset print quality.

Let's look at the pros and cons of both.

POD Pros

Low initial investment.
Easy to set up.
No storage, handling, and shipping.
It saves time you can use for marketing or writing the next book
No keeping inventory
Fully automated—the listing shows on Amazon and other online retailers within days of approving the files.
Never run out of books.
Revisions are possible. It's easy to rectify formatting mistakes.

POD Cons

Quality isn't great

The printing cost is higher than offset printing, which means a lower profit margin.

There is no discount for quantity.

There is no option to customize end sheets.

Offset Pros

Better quality paper and color.

Customized end sheet.

Lower cost of print—higher profit margin.

Offset Cons

High upfront cost

It needs storage space.

You handle shipping and handling. That's added cost and time.

There's no way to rectify mistakes in the print. No revisions once the books are printed.

Traditional publishers use offset printing for a reason. Weigh your options and the risk you're willing to take.

One option is to "test the waters" with POD, then jump all in with offset printing.

If you decide to print your books in bulk, you will be the one creating the Amazon listing. More on that in the next section.

Chapter 15 Fundraising

If you decide to do offset printing, Kickstarter is a great option to raise your initial investment. Kickstarter is a fundraising platform perfect for creators. You'll need to present your cause in the most appealing way to attract more pledges. Most successful campaigns (virtually all I've seen) have a compelling video presenting the book, the author, and the cause.

The cause is why your book is important and needed.

Look at the current Kickstarter campaigns and note what the successful ones have in common.

Once you earn the funds you need to print your books, everything that comes from their sales afterward is a bonus. Kickstarter is an all-or-nothing platform. You must set a reasonable and reachable goal, as failing to do so will result in losing all pledges.

GoFundMe works similarly to Kickstarter. It's a popular choice because you don't lose your pledges if you don't achieve your goal.

Chapter 16 Print-on-Demand Options

Ingram Spark

Ingram Spark is the most popular POD for hardcover children's books. The set-up is easy. You need to generate cover temples for your Hardcover and Paperback. Once you upload the titles, a proof copy will be generated, and you'll approve it. Make sure you're completely satisfied with the book because once you approve the files, you have to pay a revision fee to change them.

Ingram Spark gives you the option to set your book up for preorders.

KDP

Kindle Direct Publishing (KDP) is Amazon's print-on-demand press. Currently, they only offer paperbacks and Kindle for Picture books. They do offer very limited trims for Hardcovers with a minimum of 72 pages.

If you elect to be in Kindle Select, you can offer your Kindle book for free for five days out of every ninety days. The Free Kindle Days are a great promotional tool.

I use KDP in addition to Ingram Spark. I would put the Hardcover and Paperback books on pre-order through Ingram and the digital book through KDP. Then, on release day, I press the publish button on KDP for the paperback.

Other POD platforms

To be completely thorough, I have to mention that there are other options for POD.

While Ingram Spark and KDP are the most popular platforms and the ones I have personal experience with, other POD companies offer the same or similar services. My research on those options showed the following results:

Companies offering POD for print editions:

Lulu: better quality with a higher cost per book.
BookBaby: high set up fee, high cost per book.
BookVault: printing mainly in the UK. Good quality with different options not offered by others, like spiral and coil.
Blub: no setup fee, average cost per book.
Barnes and Noble Press: low royalties, quality comparable to Ingram Spark.

Digital Books:

Draft2digital: great way to distribute to all platforms selling digital books.

Kobo: more popular in Canada than in the US

Apple Books: for Apple devices only.

Google Play: offers 70% royalties on all books but has smaller US market share.

A note on using other digital book platforms in addition to KDP: selling your digital book through different platforms is called "going wide," and to do this, you can't be in Amazon Select. That means your book will not be in Kindle Unlimited and will not have the option to run Free Promo days.

Most indie authors start with being exclusive to Amazon until they gain popularity and reviews.

Linking the different formats

Once all the editions of your book show up on Amazon, they will automatically link within 72 hours. If that doesn't happen, email Amazon and ask them to link the different formats. That way, they'll be easy to find, and all editions will share the reviews.

Chapter 17 Ingram Spark Title Set-up.

I want my books to be available through all online retailers and small bookstores. That is why I offer the paperback through IS—the compensation is better than using KDP-wide distribution (which is only available for certain formats anyway.) On the other hand, I like the quality of KDP paperbacks better than the one coming out of IS press. And that is the reason I set up my paperbacks through IS and KDP at the same time. Some authors have problems using the same ISBN through Ingram **after** uploading the book to KDP first. I set up my Ingram titles before my KDP ones to avoid that. I use the same ISBN for my IS and KDP paperback versions. As long as it's the same book, you should not have a problem.

Let's go through Ingram's set-up process.

Prepare your files in advance. download a custom cover template using their cover generators.
After creating your account, choose **Upload a Title**, then **Print Book Only**.

Indicate that you have the files ready and continue. Choose **Print and Distribute** unless you only want to print copies and not make them available for sale online.

Title Information
Title of the book

Language: The primary language of the book

ISBN: Purchase and use your own ISBN. If you use the one provided for free, your book will be published by Indy Pub (Ingram Spark's imprint.)

Publishing Rights: do you owe the rights or have written permission to use the content? Is it the original work, or are you using the public domain?

Has Artificial Intelligence been used in the creation of this work?

Click on the drop-down menu. Show more fields to improve book optimization. You can include the **book subtitle** if you have one or/and the **series name** if your book is part of one.

Authors & Contributors: Author(s), Illustrator, Editor(s)

Categorize Your Title

- Imprint or Publisher's name
- Subject – use the search to find subjects related to your book
- Select Audience – age, and grade

Title Description: The book blurb that will be shown on the resellers' sites.

Keywords: search terms that customers might use to find your book.

Print Information

Select the trim size.

Interior paper and color: Is your book black-and-white or full color? For Picture Books, choose premium color and thickness.

Binding: Hardcover or Paperback.

Case laminate for Hardcover and Perfect Bound for Paperback.

You can pick between gloss and matte covers. It's a personal choice, depending on your vision and style.

After entering the **Page Count**, you will be able to see the print cost for the book.

Enter the **Price and Discount** for each territory.

A note on returns: I do not allow returns on my books for many reasons. I've heard horror stories about vast quantities of returned books months after purchase. Some bookstores would order too many copies because they know they would be able to return them, and eventually, they do. If your primary market is Amazon, there is no need to enable returns. I would rather lose a few sales than pay for hundreds or thousands of returned books.

A note on discount: there is no need to offer a bigger discount than the minimum required. As with the above, if Amazon is your primary market, you lose more than you can gain by lowering your discount.

Print Options: Here, you can allow a **look inside the book**. It's a nice perk that might convince your customers to buy your book.

Print Release Day: Pick your publication day, set your book for pre-orders, or publish it immediately.

On-sale date: the date the press begins shipping books to retailers. Allow ample time for retailers to stock up before release. You want your book to be available on release day.

Print Upload: you need two PDF files. One is the inside pages, and the other is the cover (hopefully, you downloaded and used their template.)

The system will validate your metadata and files, and if there are no errors, you will continue to the final part, where you press the **Submit** button.

Ingram Spark recently removed its set-up fees, and revisions are free for 60 days after publication. Yay!

You will receive an email when a proof copy is generated and ready to be downloaded. If everything looks good, **approve and enable distribution.**

Chapter 18 KDP Title Set-up

Begin by opening a KDP account.

Once you have that, click on the CREATE button and choose from the options—Kindle book, paperback, or hardcover.

From here, you can also manage your series page.

Choose between a Kindle book and a paperback to begin.

You will have to go through the process for each edition.

Let's start with the Kindle book.

You will need to fill in the following information:

Language of your book

Book Title

Subtitle if any

Series: is your book a part of a series? Here, you can set up your series details. You will have the option to choose between Main content and Related content. The main content is all the books in the series. Related content is everything related to that series, like journals or if you have other books with the same characters but not part of this series.

Author: your author's name or pen name.

Contributors – illustrator, editors, and anyone you want to show as a contributor. I list the illustrator and sometimes the editor of my books.

Description is the blurb for your book that will show on Amazon.

Rights: choose between the two options. If you publish an original work (a story you wrote), you owe the copyright. If you use a public domain, you must pick the second option. You have to identify your territory rights because each country's copyright duration is different.

Primary Audience: indicate your targeted age and grade.

Primary marketplace: choose your primary market (mine is Amazon.com.)

Categories: Choose three categories where your book fits best: research similar books and the categories they are listed in. Publisher Rocket is an excellent tool for that, or you can always go on Amazon and look at the categories and the books that show under each. For your Kindle book, consider categories under "Children's eBooks."

Keywords: fill the seven boxes with search terms related to your book. Consider what parents might type in Amazon if they search for a book like yours. One way to do a keyword search is to begin typing in the Amazon search box, and you get a drop-down menu of the most searched terms. Publisher Rocket is an excellent tool for that, too.

Pre-order: here, you can list your book before the publication date and make it available for pre-order or publish it immediately.

Click **Save and Continue**.

Manuscript: You can choose to protect your book by checking the DMR box, but that might prevent your book from showing correctly for some of your readers. It is your choice if you want to do that or not. If someone is set on stealing your content, they will find a way, so I don't bother with that.

Upload your file. I use Kindle Kids Create to prepare the Mobi file for Kindle. The program is free to download and easy to use.

Kindle eBook Cover: upload an image of your cover in JPEG or TIFF format.

AI-Generated Content: indicate if you use AI to generate any portion of your book.

Kindle eBook Preview: launch the previewer and make sure your book displays as you intend it to.

Kindle eBook ISBN: Kindle books do not need ISBN, but do include your Indicate the Publisher's name here.

Save and Continue

KDP Select Enrollment: it's optional but necessary if you want your book to be in Kindle Unlimited and you are planning to run free promos

Territories: I have world rights to the English versions of all my books, and I assume that is the case for you, too, unless you have signed off on your rights for specific regions. Indicate territory if you are using public domain.

Primary Marketplace: Amazon.com is the default

Pricing, royalty, and distribution: Pick 70% royalty and insert the US price; the rest will be automatically included based on your US price. You can adjust each territory if needed or leave them as they are.

Submit!

And that's it.

Now, let's look at the **paperback.**

Click on **Create a Paperback** under the same title, and most of the information, like author, contributors, and description, will be automatically transferred to that edition. You will have to choose three **categories** here, too, and they can be slightly different than your Kindle versions. For one, some of the categories under Children's Books do not match the Children's eBooks exactly, and most importantly, choosing slightly different categories gives you the option to show your book in more places. Adjust your keywords for the same reasons.

You cannot set up a pre-order for paperback on KDP. You can set up your title to be published on a day in the future, but the book would not show up till that day. Use IS to set up pre-orders for paperbacks and hardcovers.

ISBN: you can use the ISBN provided by KDP or your own. I do not recommend using the one supplied by KDP because you cannot use it anywhere else (it will be a different edition than your Ingram Spark's), and KDP will be your publisher. Purchase and use your ISBN.

Print Option:

Choose your **trim size**. The default is 6x9. Click on select a different size and pick from the options. You can also input custom sizes here.

Bleed options: choose bleed.

Cover options: matte or gloss – your choice.

Manuscript: upload a PDF file with the inside pages of your book.

Cover: Choose the option to upload a cover you already have. The cover file is a separate PDF from the interior pages and contains a double spread of your cover. Make sure you check the box if you have a barcode included on the cover.

Like with the Kindle eBook, Amazon will ask if you used AI to create any part of your book.

Launch Preview and make sure the book looks good.

On the next page, you will set up your prices and have the option to request a **Proof Copy**.

Metadata

Understanding the power of book metadata is essential. Search engines rely on this information to effectively catalog, discover, and sell your book. The main elements of book metadata, such as the title, subtitle, author's name, book description, search terms, publication date, and ISBN, allow you to optimize your book's visibility and accessibility. This control empowers you to shape your book's online presence and reach your target audience.

A crucial element of your book marketing and sales strategy is making your book easy to categorize and discover. Picking the right keywords and writing a good description can help the book's visibility and discoverability. You should select highly specific keywords to ensure your book appears first when customers search using those terms. Well-thought-out metadata ensures the book reaches its target audience, supports marketing efforts, and drives sales.

Publishing your book checklist:

Decide if you are printing in bulk or using a POD press

Send the files to your printer or upload your book to your POD press

Upload a digital edition

Once they are all live on Amazon, link the different editions

GETTING YOUR BOOK IN THE HANDS OF THE READER

In this part, we will look into how to make your book available on Amazon and other retailers of your choice. And explore the other most common avenues for sales.

Chapter 19 Selling on Amazon

If you choose the POD path, your books will be automatically listed on Amazon and other online retailers like B&N.com, Target, and Walmart. They will also be available to independently-owned bookstores and libraries to purchase directly from Ingram Spark.

If you print your books offset in larger quantities, you must list them on Amazon, providing book details and a price and managing inventory.

Let's take a look at the different Amazon programs for sellers.

KDP

Once you upload your files to KDP, they handle the rest: listing on Amazon, printing, and distributing the book. You chose three categories in which you want your book and have the option to enhance your product page on Amazon with graphics—this is called A Content. You also have the option to boost your visibility through ads.

You can run Free Promo Days or Kindle Countdown Deal for your Kindle book if you choose to be in Kindle Select. If you elect to be in Kindle Select, your digital book will be exclusive to Amazon. You cannot offer the digital copy through any other retailer. In exchange your book will be in Kindle Unlimited (KU) and available to read for free to all KU subscribers.

Another benefit of the Free Kindle Promo is that it allows potential customers to preview your book before ordering a hard copy for their kids.

Amazon Advantage just recently opened again for new accounts.

Amazon Advantage is a program geared specifically towards creators. Amazon pays you 45% of the cover price, no matter what they sell your book for. And they slash prices down, which in turn brings more sales. This is the real advantage of the program. You always get 45% of your cover price even when your books are on sale.

Amazon sends you a Purchase Order, and you're responsible for shipping the books to them. The downfall is that sometimes Amazon sends orders for just one book, which can get expensive.

Amazon will handle the shipping to customers, and your book will be available using the highly sought-after Amazon Prime shipping method.

You can enhance your product page with A Content and run ads through that program.

Seller Central is the main Amazon selling platform. Here, you decide your price, and if you reduce it, your profit will be reduced. Seller Central has the option for Ads, but books are not eligible to be served. You can fulfill your orders yourself or choose Fulfillment By Amazon (FBA), which will qualify your books for free Prime shipping.

Seller Central offers two selling plans.

Individual plan - you'll pay $0.99 per sold item.

Professional plan - $39.99 monthly, no matter how many items you sell.

Selling through Seller Central involves additional costs, such as referral, fulfillment, and storage fees.

Amazon Vendor Central is for manufacturers and distributors on a bigger scale. It's by invitation only.

Amazon Author Central

No matter how you sell on Amazon, you need to create your Author profile and claim all your books. Amazon Author Central is a great place to check your Amazon ranking, change your book description, and add your bio. Customers can follow you and be notified about your new releases.

Chapter 20 Selling Through Your Website

You should set up an eCommerce shop and sell your books through your website, too, even if you print on demand. It's smart business to have different avenues. Putting all your baskets in Amazon can be risky. Amazon is known to change policies way too often.

Setting up your own little shop allows you to sell additional merchandise connected to your book—clothes, plush toys, mugs, key chains, etc. You can also ship promotional bookmarks or fliers with your book, presenting your other offerings.

And you can offer books signed by the author—a nice touch that many people value.

You have better profit margins by selling through your website.

There are many positives to selling through your website, but you have to give your customers incentives or additional perks to buy from you instead of Amazon.

Chapter 21 Schools and In-Person Events

Schools can be a lucrative source of revenue for children's book authors.

There are several ways to earn money from school visits. For one, schools have a budget for visiting authors, and you can be compensated a reading fee for your time. I can't tell you how many authors make most of their income from school visit fees.

If you're not charging a fee for your visit, you can ask for a guaranteed number of sales. Schools that do not have the budget to pay for your time would gladly accommodate a request like that.

Ideally, you will be able to do both—receive a fee for the visit and be able to sell your book.

Begin by reaching your local schools and then widening the reach. Look for schools that strongly focus on literacy and reading programs.

Contact the right person. Typically, this would be the school librarian, reading coordinator, or teacher. Send a professional email introducing yourself and your work, explaining the benefits of your visit, and providing potential dates and times.

Always strive to offer value: outline what you can provide during your visit. This could include a reading session, a writing workshop, a Q&A session, or interactive activities related to your book.

Typically, you will do a few short readings in front of different classes with kids of various grades and ages. Tailor your presentation to the age group you'll be addressing. Plan a mix of activities to keep students engaged. This could include reading excerpts from your book, showing illustrations, and discussing the story's themes. Be prepared with activity sheets or discussion points.

After the visit, a simple thank you email to the school staff can go a long way toward building lasting relationships.

Other in-person events

Town markets, bookstore readings, and library readings are good ways to build connections and sell books.

Readers love meeting and supporting their local authors. Many bookstores are eager to host author events. Offer to do a reading, a book signing, or a workshop. Libraries often host reading programs and author visits.

Look for local fairs and community events where you can set up a booth, sell your books, and interact with potential readers.

Thoughtfully planning and executing school visits and in-person events can create memorable experiences that inspire young readers and enhance your profile as a children's book author.

YOUR MARKETING PLAN

Now, you have your files ready. You've formatted the text and the illustrations, obtained LCCN, and filed for copyright. Next is setting a release date. Don't rush the release of your book unless you have completed the following steps while doing all the other work involved in creating the book. Your marketing begins months before the publication of your book.

Chapter 22 Website

First, you have to decide if you want to use your company's (imprint) or your personal name for your website and social media. Another option is your book or book series name. Once again, think long-term and consider what is the most prudent for you.

My website is dedonibooks.com, IG – @dedoni_books.

My last name is rather long, and people often misspell it, so I wanted something shorter for my digital presence.

Building a website is a delicate task. We often gravitate towards aesthetically pleasing or inventive looks. However, the main reason people visit any website is to find the information they seek.

Keep it simple, and make sure your website visitors do not have to look hard to find information about your book, how to purchase it, about you, and contact info. Choose functionality over looks.

Adding a blog is a great way to develop your credibility and improve your site's SEO (search engine optimization—making it easier to find).

If you have a clear idea of how your website should look, you can create it yourself with one of the "drag-and-drop" website builders like Wix, Squarespace, and Weebly. Those are geared towards beginners. WordPress is more complex and requires some coding knowledge and skills.

If you're not confident in your design abilities, you can hire someone to do it for you.

I chose to invest time and learn to do it by myself so I could implement minor or major changes whenever I wanted or needed to. This is important to me because I don't want to rely on someone else. You can probably already tell that I'm a little bit of a control freak already.

But I understand that that might not be important for you, or computers, no matter how user-friendly, aren't your thing, or you chose to leave it to the professionals and decide to hire someone for that.

Things the website needs to have:
Book information.
About the Author.
Contact Information.

Email sign-up option.

Optional: if your area of expertise is related to your children's book, include some useful information for parents or educators.

Make sure your website is mobile-friendly. I'm not going to tell you how many times I have noticed one of my pages not showing right on the phone, and I would rush to fix it.

Add social media buttons to direct your visitors to your Facebook, Instagram, and Twitter profiles.

Update regularly. Keep readers informed about upcoming book signings, readings, and events.

Include direct links to purchase your books on platforms like Amazon and B&N.com.

Provide downloadable media kits with your bio, book summaries, and high-resolution images for press and bloggers. ⁇

Optimize your website for search engines (SEO) by using relevant keywords, meta descriptions, and alt text for images.

Set up Google Analytics to track website traffic, user behavior, and other valuable metrics.

Chapter 23 Social Media

Begin working on your social media presence in advance and introduce yourself as a future author. A simple introduction will do, and as the work on your book progresses, you will have more to add, such as behind-the-scenes and sneak peeks of the illustrations—anything to keep your audience excited about your book.

I like to make my posts for the month in advance at once. Your page should include posts related to your book. I say "related" because if your book is all you post about, it becomes more spam than successful marketing. Post information about your area of expertise or information connected to your book.

To gain followers, you need to be able to connect with them and provide value. That can be helpful information, entertaining posts, or posts people feel emotionally drawn to. The rule is you can promote yourself once every five posts. But if done smartly, you can promote yourself with each post without making it look like a promotion.

If your book is about mothers and you post a quote about moms, you have already put your followers in the mood to think in that direction.

I like to make different types of posts to mix and match. I usually use quotes on subjects related to my books or about kids and reading in general, "Top Five" types of posts, and either a sneak peek from a book coming soon, one of my quotes, or something I'm currently offering—free resources or sales.

You should vary your posts but keep them in the same big theme connected to your book or area of expertise.

Here's where your advertising budget comes in. You can boost your boost posts to reach and gain more followers interested in your content.

In essence, you're paying Facebook or Instagram to show your content to more people who might be interested in your work. Done right, you'll gain followers who might turn into customers.

Start small—one to three dollars a day, and test which posts bring you the most followers.

Experiment with different content and different target audiences.

The more you connect to your intended audience BEFORE the book launch, the more successful your launch will be. Marketing a book starts at least six months before its publication date.

Don't worry if you don't have many followers or subscribers yet. The important thing is that you're building it. Post about your new release and Free Promo Days.

Download the 35 Social Media Post Ideas from my website: https://www.dedonibooks.com/resources

Chapter 24 When to Run Ads

Amazon Ads

I like to wait for release day and at least 20 reviews before beginning to run Amazon Ads for my book. Amazon is the biggest book marketplace, and Amazon Ads allow you to show your book to potential customers. There are many different strategies for running ads on Amazon. It depends on your budget and risk tolerance and which strategy you want to utilize. Amazon Ads will only work for you if you have a great product and place it in front of the right audience.

The good news is that no matter which Amazon account you have—Advantage or KDP—you can run ads for all your books. KDP used to limit the ads to only books published through them, but that's no longer the case as long as your books are all claimed under your Amazon Author Central Account. From there, you can go under Reports and Marketing and access the ads console.

Facebook and Instagram Ads

Facebook and Instagram Ads are another option to show your product to potential customers.

But remember, most people do not look for products to buy on Facebook. Unlike Amazon, people aren't already in a shopping mood while they scroll through social media. While on social media, a potential customer needs to see your product more times to take action, and you're paying for impressions, which can be expensive.

There are some pros to social media ads: you have the option of creating your own eye-grabbing graphics, and it's great for brand awareness.

I have more success using Instagram ads to build my following than selling products.

Chapter 25 Email List

Every children's books author needs an email list because it's a direct line of communication with your most engaged readers—parents, educators, and librarians who are invested in your work. An email list allows you to share updates about new releases, events, and special promotions directly with your audience, fostering a loyal fan base. It also provides valuable insights into your readers' preferences, helping you tailor your content and marketing efforts effectively. In a world where social media algorithms constantly change, an email list ensures that your message reaches those who care most about your books.

Start building your email list early. Include a pop-up box on your website to collect emails. Offer something to entice people to sign up—a free book at launch, coloring sheets, or lesson plans.

A great way to collect emails is to include QR codes with a link to your email list at the end of your book along with a request for review.

Another way to build up your email list is to sign up for Bookfunnel, which offers free resources in exchange for emails. Bookfunnel works well because you can send people there directly and participate in group promos where other authors share your book or resources with their followers.

Don't forget to include a link to a sign-up form on your social media, too.

On your sign-up form, explain what they are getting in exchange for their email—a free book, activity sheets, or maybe classroom recourses. Set the expectation and fulfill it. The rule for email marketing is the same as social media posts: one in five can be promotional. The others need to deliver content your subscribers will find useful or entertaining. That is called delivering value. The main goal of your newsletter is to create a relationship with your subscribers. Building those genuine connections is how you build faithful superfans.

Chapter 26 Reviews and Launch Teams

How do you make your selections on Amazon? I look at the ratings, and I bet you do that, too. Reviews on Amazon give credibility to your book. There are different ways to obtain your initial reviews. But first, a note on Amazon Reviews: Amazon has a very strict policy regarding reviews. **You cannot pay for reviews. You cannot swap reviews with other authors or request a certain type of review. You cannot require reviews; you can only encourage your readers to leave honest reviews.**

Launch Team

Now, let's talk about the ways to get your first reviews.

Here is where your Launch Team comes in place. Your Launch Team is a group of dedicated readers willing to leave reviews in exchange for a free digital book called an Advanced Reader Copy (ARC).

The most common two ways to form a Launch Team are either to collect emails through an online form and then email your team or create a Facebook page specially for your team and post your updates there.

The Facebook page approach keeps people more involved, but you will still have to collect their email and deliver their advance reading copy as a PDF.

People sign up for Launch Teams because they want to help the author and because they receive a free book in exchange for their help. You can email them a PDF with your book or schedule a free Kindle promotion through KDP. I do both at the same time.

The PDFs I send are typically with a watermark and lower quality than the copies I use for the printers. That way, I can prevent people from stealing my work and publishing it as their own.

Only 10-30% of the people who sign up will leave reviews. If you want 20 reviews, you must have at least 50 people on your team. That's what I aim for.

Email your Launch Team on release day or post in your Facebook group dedicated to your launch.

Send your Advanced Readers Copies out and ask your team to leave their reviews. Once again, you cannot require them to do so, but you can encourage them.

At the same time, run your Free Kindle Promo days.

Schedule your Free Kindle Promo in advance. A quick note: your book has to be published before you can schedule a free promo. It cannot be done while the book is on pre-order.

Use paid services to reach more readers. There are many newsletter services offering free and bargain books. Look at their readership numbers and pick the ones with an established children's audience.

<u>Services I have used successfully:</u>
The Fussy Librarian
The eReader Café
FreeBooksy
BookBub—the book needs to be approved. Best results so far.

Post about your promotion in groups for authors you have already been active in and have established connections with. Authors help each other but need to see that you're a contributing member of their tribe.

Chapter 27 Pre-orders and Press Releases

Pre-orders

With KDP, you can set up preorders for Kindle books but not paperbacks. Paperback and Hardcover preorders can be set up through Ingram Spark. I like to do that because it lets my readers know what's next.

Press release.

Ideally, you'll send these out months before your release date. Find the contacts for your local media and email them with your press release. You can also use paid services like Newswire or Send2press to distribute your press releases. Look for magazines or periodicals that publish materials connected to the subject of your book and get in contact with those. Relevance and news worth are what journalists are looking for.

<u>Marketing Plan Checklist</u>

Website: 2-6 months before release

Social Media: 2-6 months before release.

Bonus materials: coloring pages, activity sheets, lesson plans – at release or given before that as a teaser

Launch Team: a month before release.

Scheduling Kindle Free Promo days: the book has to be published.

Press Release: 2-6 months before release.

Amazon Author Page: after the book is listed on Amazon.

RESOURCES

For ready-to-use templates that can help with your publishing journey, visit

https://www.dedonibooks.com/resources

Check out THE INDIE CHILDREN'S BOOK AUTHOR on Patreon for the latest on Writing, Publishing, and Marketing.

https://www.patreon.com/dedonibooks

Analytics:
https://analytics.google.com/
https://www.hootsuite.com

Barcode generators:
https://bookow.com

Book description generator and a QR generator:
https://kindlepreneur.com

Copyright Office:
https://www.copyright.gov/registration/

Digital books creation:
Kindle Kids Book Create – Children's Books
Kindle Create – longer works

Digital books distribution:
https://www.draft2digital.com
https://www.kobo.com
https://authors.apple.com/publish
https://play.google.com/books/publish/u/0/
https://bookfunnel.com – file distribution and email collection

Email marketing services:
https://mailchimp.com
https://www.mailerlite.com
https://convertkit.com
https://www.authoremail.com

Facebook groups for indie children's book authors:
Children's Book Authors and Illustrators: publishing, marketing and selling
20BooksForKids
Children's Book Author Community
Publishing Children's Books: an Author Community

Children's Book Author Social Media Marketing

Facebook manuscript swap groups:
Sub It Club CRITIQUE PARTNER MATCHUP—for all kinds of manuscripts

Sub It Club—active for children's books. Not only can you find someone to critique your work, but also a lot of helpful information on writing.

KIDLIT411 MANUSCRIPT SWAP—very active for Picture Books

The Writing Gals Critique Group—mostly longer works.

Formatting software:
Adobe InDesign
Scrivener
Microsoft Word
Vellum (Mac only)
Atticus
Reedsy Book Editor
Calibre
Affinity Publisher

Freelance sites:
https://reedsy.com

https://www.upwork.com

https://www.fiverr.com

https://www.freelancer.com

Illustration and Design Tools:

https://www.adobe.com/products/illustrator.html

https://procreate.com

ISBN:

US: https://www.bowker.com/isbn-us

UK: https://www.nielsenisbnstore.com/Home/Isbn

Canada: https://library-archives.canada.ca/eng

Australia: https://www.bowker.com/isbn-au

Library of Congress Control Number:

https://www.loc.gov/publish/pcn/news/index.html

Marketing materials and mockups:

https://www.canva.com

https://placeit.net

POD for print editions:

https://kdp.amazon.com

https://www.ingramspark.com

https://www.lulu.com
https://www.bookbaby.com
https://bookvault.app
https://www.blurb.com
https://press.barnesandnoble.com

Press release distribution.

https://www.send2press.com
https://www.newswire.com

Promo Sites:

https://www.thefussylibrarian.com
https://theereadercafe.com
https://www.freebooksy.com
https://www.bookbub.com

Website-building platforms:

https://www.wix.com
https://www.squarespace.com
https://www.weebly.com
https://wordpress.com
https://www.shopify.com
https://www.godaddy.com

Writing communities and forums:

https://www.scbwi.org

https://www.kidlit411.com

https://www.12x12challenge.com

Writing tools:

https://www.rhymezone.com

https://app.grammarly.com

https://prowritingaid.com

If you found this book helpful, please take a moment and leave a review on Amazon or Goodreads!

Your feedback is deeply appreciated!

Next in the series:

MARKETING CHILDREN'S BOOKS FOR INTROVERTS

A Practical Guide to Digital Marketing

www.ingramcontent.com/pod-product-compliance
Lightning Source LLC
Chambersburg PA
CBHW070112080526
44586CB00013B/1275